See How We Grow

by Katacha Diaz

Editorial Offices: Glenview, Illinois • Parsippany, New Jersey • New York, New York

Sales Offices: Needham, Massachusetts • Duluth, Georgia • Glenview, Illinois
Coppell, Texas • Sacramento, California • Mesa, Arizona

Samantha and Serena Shimada are twins. And like children everywhere, the twin sisters are growing and changing all the time. Come along and see!

Samantha and Serena spend most of their time sleeping and eating. Mama and Papa feed the twins warm milk from a bottle. Samantha and Serena eat the same food at every meal. That's a lot of milk!

Like most babies, Samantha and Serena are very little. When they cry, being held and gently cuddled make the twins feel better.

Samantha and Serena learn something new all the time. They like to look at Mama and Papa. And they learn to smile, coo, and babble too!

Now that Samantha and Serena are older and stronger, they learn to push themselves across the floor. Soon the baby twins are on the move and crawling!

Samantha and Serena are growing all the time. Look! Can you see how Samantha and Serena are growing and changing all the time?

As the twins keep growing, Samantha and Serena learn to do more new things. They learn to sit up and stand.

Samantha and Serena learn to take small steps. The twins' legs are a bit wobbly at first. Samantha and Serena keep practicing until they walk on their own. Now the twins are really on the move!

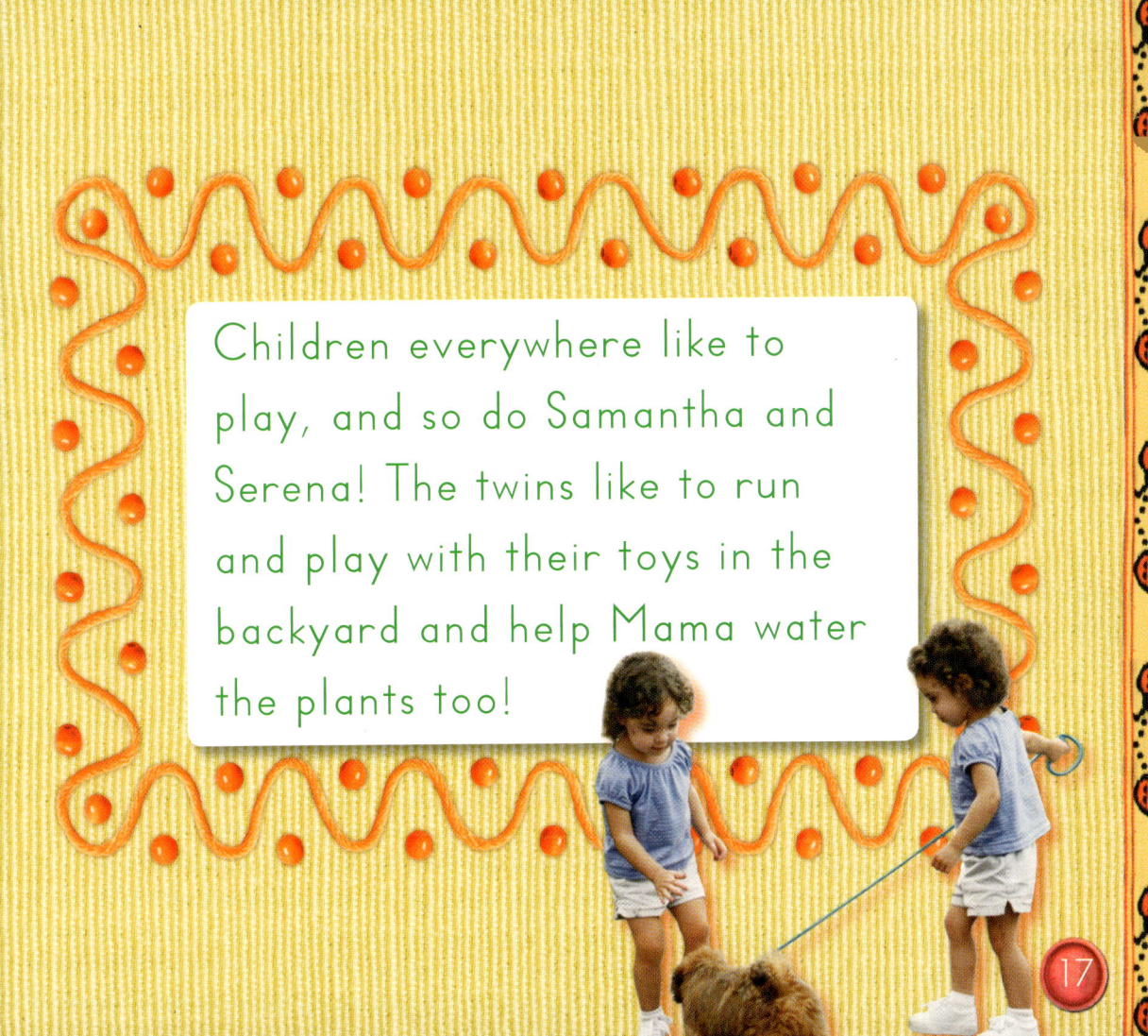

Children everywhere like to play, and so do Samantha and Serena! The twins like to run and play with their toys in the backyard and help Mama water the plants too!

Now that Samantha and Serena are older and can talk, it is easier for Mama and Papa to figure out what is wrong when they cry.

It's fun to see how much Samantha and Serena have grown and changed! Samantha and Serena are just like you and children everywhere!

Samantha and Serena are still growing and changing, and learning new things all the time. Look at pictures to see what you were like as a baby. And you will see how much you have grown and changed too!